Poems

First published in 2011 by
Liberties Press
Guinness Enterprise Centre | Taylor's Lane | Dublin 8
Tel: +353 (1) 415 1224
www.libertiespress.com | info@libertiespress.com

Trade enquiries to Gill & Macmillan Distribution
Hume Avenue | Park West | Dublin 12
T: +353 (1) 500 9534 | F: +353 (1) 500 9595 | E: sales@gillmacmillan.ie

Distributed in the UK by
Turnaround Publisher Services
Unit 3 | Olympia Trading Estate | Coburg Road | London N22 6TZ
T: +44 (0) 20 8829 3000 | E: orders@turnaround-uk.com

ISBN: 978-1-907593-17-8

2 4 6 8 10 9 7 5 3 1
A CIP record for this title is available from the British Library.

Design by spacecreative.ie
Printed and bound by CPI Group (UK) Ltd, Croydon, CR0 4YY

The publishers gratefully acknowledge financial assistance from the Arts Council.

Poems

Maurice Craig

Selected and edited by Andrew Carpenter
With an introductory essay by Lucy Collins

Contents

Preface   7

*The Poetry of Maurice Craig: 'One Sharp Stab
    of Time' by Lucy Collins*   9
A matter of orchestration   21
Storm   22
After summer's ruin   23
All down the placid surface   25
At the stone circle   26
Autumn song   27
Easter Tuesday 1941   28
Kilcarty to Dublin, 1942   29
'Peace is but an accident'   30
Spring 1943   31
Talk with an astronomer   32
Georgian Dublin   33
Merrion Square: A descriptive poem   34
Appointed to be sung in churches   40
High on a ridge of tiles   41
Ballad to a traditional refrain   42
Three cat-poems   43
On the demolition of Coole House   44
The pictures in the gallery   45
Three epigrams   46
Poem for myself   47
Sitting beside the fire alone   48
Proverbial poem   49
Two voyages   50
No climate for the vulture   51
First winter   52
These grassy walks   53

Against rhetoric in love   54
Although the lustre of your hair   55
Fire! Fire!   56
Flowers upon your lips and hands   57
The kiss   58
Inside and out   59
Love-poem   60
Poem for Linde   61
A habit or, 'Emotion recollected in tranquillity'   62
To his beloved on her having furnished
       his room with curtains   63
You whom I know   64
The false start   65
To the house of my hosts in October   66
Marlay Park   67
A diary-entry versified   68

Notes   71

Preface

Maurice Craig, Ireland's most distinguished architectural historian, was born in Belfast in 1919 and educated in Dalkey, County Dublin and at Shrewsbury School. After three years at Magdalene College Cambridge, to which he had won a scholarship, he returned to Ireland, where he gained a doctorate from Trinity College Dublin for his work on the prose-writer and poet Walter Savage Landor.

Though he is best known for his books of architectural history – *The Dublin Churches* (1948), the celebrated *Dublin 1660-1860* (1952 and several subsequent editions), *Classic Irish Houses of the Middle Size* (1976, 2006) and *The Architecture of Ireland* (1982) – Maurice has also made lasting contributions in other disciplines. His life of Lord Charlemont, *The Volunteer Earl* (1948), and his *Irish Bookbindings 1660-1800* (1954) remain unsurpassed, while his anthology *Cats and their Poets* (2002), his collection of *100 Poems by W. S. Landor*, his whimsical autobiography *The Elephant and the Polish Question* (1990) and his fascinating *Mausolea Hibernica* (1999, 2009), produced in collaboration with his son Michael, have given delight to many. His prose style is famous for its elegance and wit, and his books and articles for deep learning lightly worn.

As a young man, Maurice was a prolific and highly respected poet, and the purpose of this selection from his poems is to introduce them to a new generation of readers. The majority of the poems printed here are from his book *Some Way for Reason* (1948), but others come from his holograph manuscripts. All except 'Marlay Park' were written between 1939 and about 1947.

I should like to thank Maurice for his willing endorsement of this venture, for making his manuscripts available to me, for giving permission for the printing or reprinting of his poems, and for helping me to gloss some obscure allusions.

Many thanks also to Lucy Collins for her introductory essay and for assistance throughout the project, and to Michael and Gemma Craig for many fine lunches.

Andrew Carpenter
Dalkey, January 2011

The Poetry of Maurice Craig: 'One Sharp Stab of Time'

I

It is hard not to look on Irish and British poets of the 1940s as a lost generation, overshadowed on one side by the giants of Modernism – Eliot and Pound – and on the other by the challenging diversity of later twentieth-century poetries. In both Ireland and Britain the forties was a decade of reduced poetic vigour: Yeats had died in 1939 and the ideological struggle that had animated many of the major figures of the thirties was overtaken by the crisis of World War II. In Britain, the war and subsequent economic hardship inevitably overshadowed cultural developments: poetry magazines tended to be short-lived, and the opportunities for book publication were significantly curtailed. The Irish Free State, in its turn, was unable to summon the energies of the pre-Independence period, and its insularity dampened artistic production. Yet in spite of the perception of the forties in Ireland as a depressed decade, it was in fact an important time for debates on the future of Irish art and literature. An awareness of this decade as a nexus of influences, both in political and aesthetic terms, is important for any reading of the poetry of Maurice Craig.

Craig is widely known as an architectural historian and biographer: those encountering his writing today may not even be aware that he was a poet of repute during his twenties, one expected to become a major figure on the Irish poetry scene. Yet he published just one full-length collection of poems before, in his own words, the springs of Helicon ran dry for him. Craig is modest on the subject of his literary and intellectual ability, suggesting that if you have little talent, 'you must put everything you have into whatever you do'. Misplaced though his modesty may be, this comment reveals an acute awareness of the entangled nature of creative and intellectual aims, and of the dedication required to realise them. In spite of the fact that Craig's poetry publications are few in number, his engagement with the process of writing poetry, with the perfecting of form, and with the careful editing and placement of his work in journals and anthologies, testifies to a young man of creative ambition and considerable powers of intellectual concentration.

Craig's poems began appearing in journals during the early years of the 1940s, and his pattern of publication is revealing of the magazine culture of the time. He was published in the well-established *Dublin Magazine* in 1942, where his work was placed alongside that of notable poets, many with Modernist tendencies; north of the border he appeared with some regularity in *Lagan* between 1943 and 1945. Significantly too, *The Bell* provided an important early outlet for Craig's poems, which contributed to the diversity of style and interest that the magazine wished to foster. *The Bell* cultivated a readership from all over Ireland, and its publication of work by Ulster writers demonstrated a conviction that the division brought about by partition could be overcome by cultural means. The determination of the journal's editors to create an international dimension to Irish literary culture cultivated an interest among its readers and contributors in artistic developments abroad. It was an aim in tune with Craig's poetic temperament (in 1938 he had spent a formative summer in Paris, where he visited James Joyce) and it created an inclusive framework within which to view Craig's writing.

The decades of the mid-century were particularly promising ones for Northern Irish poetry. Louis MacNeice was the most significant poet to emerge from Ulster during this time, and though he spent most of his adult life in England, MacNeice revealed new thematic and stylistic possibilities to Irish writers. The province also proved itself able to sustain a worthwhile journal culture – *Lagan* and *Rann* being notable examples – and this fostered the work of a number of poets who would make a leading contribution to Irish letters in the twentieth century: W. R. Rodgers, Robert Greacen and John Hewitt, as well as less well-known figures such as Roy McFadden and Seán Jennett. McFadden himself had strong convictions regarding the particularity of the Ulster achievement, putting forward the view that writers from the province regarded themselves as forging a tradition that was separate from the Revivalist mode in Ireland, as well as from traditions of English poetry. Besides being published in *Lagan*, Craig's poems appeared in the pamphlet *Poems from Ulster*, edited by Robert Greacen and published in Belfast in 1942. In his preface to this anthology, Greacen noted the challenges that young poets of the era faced as they strove to establish themselves in a climate of war and austerity. He remarked on the 'disintegration' of the group associated with the thirties and the recognition by a younger generation of British poets that the time was opportune for 'a return to a literature that springs out of life and reality, a literature strengthened and made more flexible by the use of traditionalist forms'. Greacen's inclusion of poems by the then twenty-two-year-old Maurice Craig exemplifies the kind of regeneration both this editor and other commentators envisaged. The apparent simplicity of these poems, and their evident dedication to formal achievement, reflect the need to respond sincerely to the crisis of the age, as well as the conviction that poetry was not superfluous to this crisis but was instead an important means by which it could be both understood and endured.

Though Craig's promise as a poet was quickly acknowledged, it took some time for this talent to be realised in the form of a full collection. His appearance in the Greacen selection of 1942 coincided with the publication of *Twelve Poems*, a privately printed gathering of his own poems published in an edition of a hundred copies. In the previous year Gayfield Press had published

Craig's poem 'Black Swans'. This 'curiously convoluted allegory', as Geoffrey Taylor described it, was part of a series of illustrated pamphlets featuring single poems by Irish poets from the Republic and from Ulster. The Gayfield enterprise was praised by reviewers, and it is indicative of the rather bleak conditions for publishing at this time, both in Britain and in Ireland, that this comparatively small-scale initiative attracted particular notice. It was a further six years before Craig's only collection, *Some Way for Reason*, appeared – not from an Irish publisher but from Heinemann in London in 1948.

As this pattern of publication might suggest, Craig occupies a complex position within the Irish poetry tradition. A Belfast Protestant, he studied at Cambridge as an undergraduate; yet the years between 1941 and 1943, when his finest poems were written, were spent in Dublin, completing a PhD at Trinity College on the early-nineteenth-century writer Walter Savage Landor. This was an important period for Craig, formative of his interest in Ireland's built environment, and of a poetics combining personal experience and serious intellectual engagement. Landor proved an important influence on Craig's poetry, but so too did the literature of his undergraduate years – both the seventeenth- and eighteenth-century poets he studied and the British and Irish poets writing and publishing during the time he spent at Cambridge. In the generation that immediately preceded his, the most important influence was Geoffrey Taylor, who was for some years poetry editor of *The Bell*. Their work would occasionally appear together in anthologies, together with contributions by poets such as Padraic Fallon, Ewart Milne and Freda Laughton. Several of these anthologies, including Devin A. Garrity's *New Irish Poets* (1948), sought to give shape to the newest work emerging from Ireland in these decades and offer insights into the relationship between Craig's work and that of his contemporaries. His most anthologised poem, however, is 'Ballad to a traditional refrain', a poem in which the most familiar line is not, in fact, Craig's own. This is a curious detail, but not an insignificant one; it reveals the telling ways in which his poetic imagination draws sustenance not just from current ideas but also from pre-existing forms. The meticulous scholar of later years is visible in these early poems, though their range of intellectual engagement is worn lightly.

Though *Some Way for Reason* was not widely reviewed, it was praised by several commentators for both its sensitivity of mood and precision of style: 'In a world where . . . the inevitable process of disintegration has spread to the arts, it is a heartening thing to meet new verse that is well-formed, meaningful, and human', Kevin Faller wrote in *Irish Book Lover*. As well as detecting Modernist influences, critics drew attention both to the objectivity and the sympathy evident in these poems. This is perhaps a strange combination, but it is a feature of Craig's poetry that he entwines the emotional and the cerebral with remarkable subtlety. Such a combination is not exclusive to Craig, of course, but its presence in his work speaks to the needs of the time – to the requirement for clear-sighted engagement with contemporary politics, as well as to the conviction that being true to one's self is ultimately a redemptive act.

II

Maurice Craig's poetry is characterised by the same love of words and the same precise care in their use that is to be found in all his writing; the formal containment to which this precision gives rise is not the result of narrowness of vision but rather of an ability to condense an entire process of questioning into a single image or turn of phrase. This epigrammatic quality does not exclude depth of feeling, though it does refrain from anatomising it. In this respect, the condensed effect of the metaphysical poets shadows Craig's work, and with it the vividness of imagery and the desire for sensory experience with which those earlier poets engaged so intensely. The satirical wit that is a feature of his poetry is, in fact, often created through the adoption of a mid-twentieth-century perspective on earlier poetic forms. 'Against rhetoric in love' disavows the use of rhetorical devices while using them to skilful effect. The choice of the sonnet alerts us immediately to the controlled energies of the form in Craig's hands. He sets up the expected turn carefully, yet the argument is for reticence in the expression of love, a reticence that is at odds with the need for closure suggested by the sonnet form itself, and with the sexual undercurrents that move finally to full expression.

Time plays an important part in almost all Craig's poems, and seasonal shifts appear repeatedly. 'The false start' develops this trope, turning attention to the hope generated by the first hints of spring. The impossibility of living in the present is the key concern – 'Anticipation, retrospect, alone/Can dwell upon the lucid interval' – reflecting both existential concerns and the uncertainties generated by war. Fittingly, perhaps, autumn is the more persistent feature, yet these poems actually lie between seasons: it is the approach of autumn and its inevitable sense of decay that poems such as 'All down the placid surface' and 'After summer's ruin' depict. The latter is one of a number of poems showing the influence of Yeats, and the older poet's sensitivity to the disintegration of order and to the loss of love resonates in Craig's work. Layers of memory exist in these poems, and the expected dissolution has already begun to happen, because its imaginative recognition proves as significant as the process itself. Interestingly, these poems adopt a freer form than many others in this book. Though both alliteration and assonance can be traced through them, there is no fixed rhyme scheme, and rhythmic patterns emerge and fade. In this way the poems suggest their own vulnerability; fixedness ultimately eludes them.

Maurice Craig's enduring interest in the way in which history is revealed in his own time and place has shaped his career as an architectural historian. It inflects these poems too, both in their reference to historical events and figures, and in his larger philosophical awareness of the ways in which the past lives in the present. His sensitivity to this layered perspective is unusual, and offers a depth of reflection that allows the poetry to transcend its moment of writing. The most remarkable of these historical works is 'Merrion Square', which, as a long poem, is unusual in Craig's oeuvre. Like its subject matter, it is elegantly proportioned and employs a suitably retrospective style of couplets, mostly in full rhyme. Politics and aesthetics are crucially juxtaposed here: the cultural 'blue-print on the green' is a built environment of great beauty and endurance 'though some might say that so/The blue mark of the bruise outlasts the blow'. This poem reinforces the classicism that is an important feature of Craig's style, with its emphasis on balance and on public concerns, yet it also draws particular attention to the perspective of the speaker. Subtitled 'A descriptive poem', it encompasses some of the styles of eighteenth-century verse, acknowledging this with a mention of James Ward's 'Phoenix Park' of 1718 in the opening stanza. By adopting aspects of its precursor's digressive structure, it permits social and cultural history to exist alongside aesthetic comment and contemporary observation. Formally too, Craig's poem expands and contracts to accommodate these shifts in perspective: stanzas range between four and eighteen lines in length, registering both the alertness and the unease of the speaker. He is, like so many of his eighteenth-century poetic counterparts, a surveyor, whose vantage-point on the streetscape he documents is a vital part of its meaning.

The centrality of Irish subject matter in this poem is significant. If 'Merrion Square' begins by asserting the importance of such a choice ('Let Irish archers choose an Irish mark'), it is indicative of the poet's own priorities:

everywhere in Craig's work the presence of Ireland emerges in subtle ways. Belfast is a recurrent feature of these poems for a number of reasons. In 'Easter Tuesday 1941' the bombing of civilian targets in Belfast forms the focus of the poet's contemplation of a beleaguered city, both parts of its divided community damaged by the attack. The subtle shifts in how rhyme is used here – both full rhyme and eye rhyme – shows all the senses under siege, while the reference to 'diggers with both feet' at once summons and transcends the religious divisions within the community. This is one of a number of poems that allude directly to World War II, which is an implicit presence in so much writing from this period. 'Kilcarty to Dublin, 1942', completed in March of that year, is a striking example of how the larger consequences of the war reverberate far from the sites of conflict. Here the details of Irish rural life are 'taken apart and sorted and shaken/By a war that rages across two seas', suggesting not the disorder of violence but its power to provoke intense reflection. If Ireland remained neutral during the war, it was nonetheless affected by the mood of uncertainty and disillusionment that prevailed.

The destructive power of violence unsurprisingly shadows many of these poems. 'Peace is but an accident' and 'Spring 1943' speak directly to European politics, and to the ways in which prolonged conflict can change our ability to judge what is normal. Here the regularity of verse form is turned to the service of this fear; its order is not redemptive but emphasises the relentless rationality of ideological aims pursued to their conclusion. There is also an enduring sense of foreboding among these poems that speaks not only of political, but also of personal, unrest. In 'Poem for Linde' these elements are intertwined: the embracing lovers overlooking the lock are mirrored in the geography of Dublin encircled by its canals. The lock's purpose in controlling the level of the water and its flow is akin to the poet's restraint in handling the poem's emotional energy, as it weighs depth of love against the hesitancy of its expression. The couple have 'but the frail revetment of our love/To match against what nightmare tidal wave?' Their precarious state does not relate only to the inevitable uncertainties of love, but to the vulnerability of individual lives set against larger powers.

This instability lies also within the singular human state – within the speaker or poet registering his own struggle towards meaning. The opening image of 'Poem for myself' is striking in this regard: the speaker ascending the stairs finds the steps behind him cancelled as he climbs. Each turn of the stair signifies a new 'episode', one that cannot find meaning through its connection with what has gone before: the unanswered question, the letter which never arrives – everything here speaks of a past that is 'irrevocably lost' yet which continues to haunt the present. That the human response to unfulfilled desire is ultimately to create a false contentment, registers again the self-deception that has been suggested in other poems. Yet the poem is also implicitly concerned with the failure of continuity, the kind of continuity that makes faith in the creative process possible. The darkness with which the poem begins sets its mood: this is an extraordinary poem for a man of twenty-three to write, not least because of the weight of experience it suggests, and its weary pacing out of full and half-rhymes. Yet it is indicative of our understanding of Maurice Craig as a poet whose work is in touch with, yet exceeds, his own experience. The synthesis of thought and feeling that is achieved in these poems is understated, both because the poet avoids declarations of heightened emotion, and because of the deceptive simplicity of so much of his work. Indeed it is our sense of what is withheld from us as readers that sharpens our engagement with these remarkable poems.

Lucy Collins

Poems

A matter of orchestration

The winter sunlight like a trumpet's note
Is tongued in triplicate above the town
And bars of brazen cloud are bright and clean.
The breathing houses lazily beneath
Confront each other on the gap-toothed quays,
Their paintwork dappled in the oily water:
The woodwind's coloured blobs supported by
The undulating groundswell of the strings.

So rich the voice that from the shell still sings.

Storm

You'd think this wind would blow the stars about,
Knock some together, even blow some out,
But not a bit of it. And here's the sea
Luminous grey and angry, making free
Of groin and natural bone, and curling up
To show white teeth, his petulant upper lip.

But this proud slave, for all his present rage
With luck may leave to a succeeding age
A little gravel somewhat finer ground.
We're but browbeaten where the sea is bound;
And some who quail before his rant and roar
Will in a score of years accomplish more.

After summer's ruin

After summer's ruin a fair-haired horseman
Reins in by the lakeside, where the russet
Leaves have lost their flesh but keep their structure
Yet between hoof and mud.
                    His glance is levelled
Over the water and one leisured swan
To the unlikely gimcrack tower that perches
Preciously on its neatly moulded mound.

Light reflected from an erratic facet
Looks out blindly at a single pane,
Picks on another, misses fire, and burns
Redder again from somewhere unforeseen.
The woods gather together, up and inwards:
A shivering of such leaves as yet remain
Strokes with a delicate fingertip the listening
Ear of the rider.
                Swivelling soundlessly
Another tapered ear is spared to take
Note of the circumstance. The rider feels
The quivering nostril, the ripple along the flank
That seems prolonged to ruffle the water and shake
The rushes at its edge.
                  Now the whole earth
Will gather suppleness, limbering up for winter,
And the man remembering himself remember
A clump-shod walker blown about the lanes,
Or daring the frozen rut to bear the boot,
Or standing when the fine rain of the spring
Has drained the wind of power, breathlessly watching
Pale evergreens pointed with water-drops.

During the next few months or so, no doubt,
A stucco slab or two may come unstuck
And drop like icing from a cake that now
No longer tempts the taste.

And now already
The rider lifts his wrist, consults the time,
Speaks in a soft voice to his horse, and both
Turn to the setting sun and so depart.

All down the placid surface

All down the placid surface of the stream
The inflated coinage of the duckweed floats,
And none knows now where lay the dragon-fly
Stunned at the trunk's foot in the drowsy air
Made heavy by the mouldering of leaves.
Loneliness widens with the widening sky
At the approach of autumn.
                              If by death
Of those who loitered here a year ago
These reaches were deserted, life could bear
Such termination.
                              But the scattering
Of stones flung far, so far that from this out
Some of their rings may never intersect,
Weighs heavier on the mind than if a flame
Struck instantaneously, and shrivelled each
To melting-point in one sharp stab of time.

At the stone circle

Almost three thousand years had past,
Before he found their sprinkled ring of stone:
A six-months' hunger drove him back at last
But this time not alone.

Since they had chosen well the place
All round the changing features looked at him;
The brutal stones slant-cut the whin-grown grass
And the horizon's rim.

Upon the floor of sacrifice
He stood alive: life looked a static thing
When he saw in the others' lips and eyes
The men who built the ring.

Autumn song

Now that an early frost
Crinkles the crackling leaves
Down at the lake's edge,
The earth in an iron ridge
Holds hard, no longer keeps
A print where she has past.

Clear sunlight at her eyes
Slants in, precise and cool.
The brittle twigs give tongue
At fracture of each prong.
Starred ice upon the pool's
Still starred at next sunrise.

Sharp-focused now to me
In aromatic places
She walks the fittest path
Across the ungrudging earth,
Forgetting the aching spaces
Of the hungry sea.

Easter Tuesday 1941

Now that death is dropping
On the quivering mud
And on the just and unjust
Falls the rain of blood
God send the flares may light you
The way out of the wood.

You never took so kindly
To parliaments or votes,
But rifles on the barricades –
More like starving stoats
Trapped in a hole, and digging
Teeth in each other's throats.

But the same aches and fevers
The same cold and heat
The same sun and shadow
The same rain and sleet
And the same death from nowhere falls
On the diggers with both feet.

Steel and concrete, floating
On the estuary bog
Rest on nothing sounder
Than a drifting log.
No burrow can protect you
From the power of a dog.

Steel and stone divide you
But their time runs late.
May you go out on the mountains
At the northern gate
Where Wolfe Tone and McCracken
Begot the Ninety-Eight.

Kilcarty to Dublin, 1942

The paraffin-lamps and the home-cured bacon
The whitewash misty behind the trees
Are taken apart and sorted and shaken
By a war that rages across two seas.
The sweets in the dim shop-window glitter
The idiot-girl still sniffs in the bus:
The literal meaning of all grows bitter
If not for her, then at least for us.
But life goes on in the last lit city
Just in the way it has always done
And pity is lost on the tongues of the witty
And the wolf at the door is a figure of fun.

'Peace is but an accident'

General Franco, 21 August 1942

All you imagined normal was only a bubble
In the material stream, and now it's burst.
The sphere it circumscribed was never stable:
An overgrown exception from the first.

Purpose and peace, as momentary illusions
Produced by an accidental trick of the light
Having nothing to do with law, have no lawful
    occasions:
Cannot go wrong, since they were never right.

But still the stream that flows through generations
Deposits foundations, tempting you to build.
Be deaf and blind to the constructive passions.
They are not part of the plan. They have not killed.

Spring 1943

The crackling laughter of malignant gods
Disturbed our sleep all winter, yet we allowed
The smoke that lent a sharpness to the air
To stand for the resurrection of the dead.
And now the brighter bonfires of the spring
Are burning, and for a time we must admire
The flaring tongues of flame that lap and lick
Around the resinous twigs, the rivulets
Of sap, that hissing load the air with scent.
And for a time, like children, we delight
In finery of destruction, we who know
The same pot boils, however fresh the thorns.

Talk with an astronomer

In this library
Where on the shelves
The plotted movements of the stars,
Their density, intensity
Remote from our intestine wars
Are stacked around and stare at me,
I give myself not whole, but still by halves.

Still the pale blue eyes
Behind the lenses,
Melodious rise and fall of a German voice
In fall or rise, not even tries
But without effort, without noise
Satisfies unterrestrial desires
To all appearance free of all our frenzies.

Stranger whom I meet
This evening only
To talk of time inside an empty space
Without the murky heat, the beat
Of trussed-up thinking; in your face
I find reflections of the feet
Whose head's more desolate than ours, more lonely.

Georgian Dublin

'So much to do,' said Turgot, 'and so little
Time to do it.' Civilisation must wait
Impotently crouching over the grate,
Watching to seize the moment, the boiling kettle;
Must grasp it suddenly, deftly, like a nettle,
Without reluctance, not too early or late,
That in the flawed alembic of the state
Correct precipitates may form and settle.

In the quick sunlight of those thirty years
This Roman Empire waited for Sedan.
Though now their building is a hollow shell,
That sea-worn tracery can move to tears.
This capital is incorruptible,
Doric, Ionic and Corinthian.

Merrion Square: A descriptive poem

The shaft of verse but rarely can transfix
The target; rarely hits, and still more rarely sticks.
Let Irish archers choose an Irish mark,
Be like James Ward who wrote the *Phoenix-Park*
Two centuries since (nor badly): and although
Few may be called to draw *Ulysses'* bow
(Whose twang reverberates yet across the sea)
I still (for one) may find here what for me
May ring the bell and shame the false alarms
From bogs and battlefields: lost faiths, lost farms.
For structures, built though but with hands and bricks,
Survive the hucksterdom of politics.

These clear November mornings light is kind:
The ebb of shadow like a slow-drawn blind
Retreats toward my point of view, and there,
Still touched with lingering mist, lies Merrion Square.
These hundred years, its builders in retreat
Have left square after square, street after street.
The buildings lasted longer than the lease:
The figures dwindle, and the frames increase;
And those who built this city for a few
Laid out the Wide Streets wider than they knew.

That flame is cold, yet still some warmth remains
In evening sunlight warped in window-panes
And brickwork glowing with a century's stains.
Some stains they left, it's true, eat through the page
On which their history's written, and the rage
That they provoked, no beauty can assuage.
The print they left, a blue-print on the green
(By then already very far from clean)
Survives them still, though some might say that so
The blue mark of the bruise outlasts the blow.
But no injustice of the past offsets

These ranks of chimneys over parapets,
Although each tributary hearth may warm
A scene so changed in all but outward form:
Stenographers in artificial silk
Type out in triplicate the price of milk;
Directors' desks ensconce the former serf,
And marble mantels are a frame for turf.

Into the unkempt gardens no-one comes
But ragged children from the neighbouring slums
Who slip through gaps prised open in the paling
Or profit by some privileged person's failing
To lock the gate behind him every time.
The small creep in, the big perhaps may climb:
In present justice, both may rank as crime.

In those two houses there (the corner ones)
Marie Reparatrice maintains her nuns,
Who constantly, in shifts, adore the Host.
They've treated the place well, compared with most:
No gold-tipped railings, hideously new,
Obtrude themselves upon the outward view.
Inside, the case is different, no doubt,
But I'm content to watch it from without
With idle eyes. The Faith parades in strength:
A file of children half a mile in length
Trundles interminably. The little mites
Are shepherded across the traffic-lights:
Like ants on the ant-eater's tongue, they crawl
Into the reticent and fanlit hall.
No harm, perhaps, is done; perhaps some good:
Of that I neither can be judge, nor would.

When evening draws the lengthening vistas out,
Distinguished spectres surely walk about
Under the trees: Yeats with his chin in air,
And Russell nestling in his beard, are there,

And spattering on his patent-leather toes
The drop still drips from Edward Martyn's nose
And Moore is fascinated still. Not I:
These, if they walk, have always passed me by.
Even the archetypal mage of all,
Sheridan Le Fanu, to whose least call
Unnumbered apparitions rose, can raise
No shadow of himself to haunt these ways.

But on the darkest night I would not shun
That unjust judge, Sir Jonah Barrington,
Although through him a heartless culture spoke,
As quick to crack a skull as crack a joke.
But ah! Sir Jonah, now 'twould give you pain
To tread the flags of Merrion Square again.
You looked upon the wine when it was red,
But claret – aye, and clarity – are fled,
Healths, hangings and hilarity . . . alack,
We look upon the stout when it is black
And grieve that it should ever come to pass
That men should see so darkly through a glass.

And dark, indeed, is all that may be seen
At night in Merrion Square and Stephen's Green.
The crowded trams that lurch along the lines
To dim Dunleary and to raw Rathmines
Plough each their wake of light. From dim-lit verge
The drab and sluttish prostitutes emerge
Flaunting and cringing each alternate yard
For Civil Servant, or for Civic Guard;
Till midnight puts a hush on everything
And cats and drunken medicals may sing.

The song that now pervades the Dublin dark
Seems calculated to provoke remark.
The Gaelic gift along the echoing street
Has found its last and least inspired retreat.

And thus it comes about that, though by day
The barrel-organists, and even harpers, play,
By night all's given over to the wail
Of youth linked arm-in-arm, as, male by male,
Female by female only, boy and girl
Lean heavily on each melodic twist and twirl.
In their slow veins the blood perhaps may run
Of her who mourned the fate of Usna's son
And Deirdre still laments, though changed the air
She sings to, as she's Moving Through The Square.

At last all's quiet; not a sound is heard
Save horn, like call of predatory bird
From far away, where carfuls of police
Patrol the empty streets to keep the peace.

A gentle mist may still caress at dawn
This bristle-tufted and unshaven lawn,
May still dissolve harsh lines, and so erase
The profile of each bush around the base,
That Leinster House, though just across the way,
Gleams faint beyond an acre of Cathay.
The lesser, too, that flank its grey with red,
Though ill-regarded, still remain well-bred.
No rigid uniformity of edge
Binds all together, yet the coping-ledge
May mask a catwalk for a lonely gun,
Give cover for a tabby on the run,
And, in the dog-days, trap the throbbing sun.
Gentility and chastity of line,
Augustan principles of street design,
May warm no other heart, and yet warm mine.

But one by one the gentle and the chaste,
Damp-rotten, are repointed and refaced
And re-emerge, as though the brickwork bled,
Touched up with slabs of raw and glossy red.

And yet the light is kind even to these,
And through the screen, even of winter trees,
With time and weather, they contrive to please.

To please? No more? It's time I should produce
Some colourable shadow of excuse
Why I, whose father in a country town
Kept, at my age, a watch on each half-crown,
Should snatch the past of others for my own,
Instal myself upon an empty throne,
And, heir-presumptive, with presumptuous air,
Survey the monarchy of Merrion Square.

This battle-cockpit of conflicting laws
Invites the occupant to seek the cause
Why every matrix of our culture broke
When put to test. We grew not as the oak
In slow concentric rings. But faggots bound
Haphazardly, the rotten with the sound,
Present our case. No talk of trees will work,
Although this country gave the world a Burke.
Or, if it must, let's call the land a graft –
Was that Sir Jonah Barrington who laughed?
I take him up. Although I meant no pun
I'll use it now in something more than fun.
Not only did the Anglo-Irish wrap
The alien slip close to the bleeding sap,
They cut the tree for firewood by-and-by
To make a blaze before the wood was dry.

And yet no other frame than theirs will suit.
Idle to scrabble for a deeper root.
Though Cashel, Devenish and Clonmacnois
May speak with almost comparable voice,
Something is lacking in the sculptured stone;
Sermons are there, but sermons there alone.
The lay layout of market-place and forum

Is secular, without the *saeculorum*.
But if the root is dead and will not grow,
And this dull fire, for all its inward glow,
Remains a cromlech hollow at the heart?
– Collapse the capstone, surfaces apart
Jumble together, that the flame may leap,
Stir up the embers from their brittle sleep
And when all's flickered to a final flash
Weigh in your palm the warm and feathery ash.
When all lies burnt and open to the skies
Who knows what future it may fertilise?

Appointed to be sung in churches

Hear how Sternhold and Hopkins, Tate and Brady,
Those staunch symmetrical psalm-singing souls,
Have rammed the round pegs of the Harp of David
Into square holes.

High on a ridge of tiles

High on a ridge of tiles
A cat, erect and lean
Looks down and slyly smiles;
The pointed ears are keen
Listening for a sound
To rise from the back-yard:
He casts upon the ground
A moment's cold regard.

Whatever has occurred
Is on so small a scale
That we can but infer
From the trembling of the tail
And the look of blank surprise
That glares out of the eyes
That underneath black fur
His face is deadly pale.

Ballad to a traditional refrain

Red brick in the suburbs, white horse on the wall,
Eyetalian marbles in the City Hall:
O stranger from England, why stand so aghast?
May the Lord in His mercy be kind to Belfast!

This jewel that houses our hopes and our fears
Was knocked up from the swamp in the last hundred years:
But the last shall be first and the first shall be last
May the Lord in His mercy be kind to Belfast!

We swore by King William there'd never be seen
An all-Irish Parliament at College Green,
So at Stormont we're nailing the flag to the mast:
May the Lord in His mercy be kind to Belfast!

O the bricks they will bleed and the rain it will weep
And the damp Lagan fog lull the city to sleep;
It's to hell with the future and live on the past
May the Lord in His mercy be kind to Belfast!

Three cat-poems

Address of welcome

Like cattle-raiding heroes of the Táin
I've made a kitten-raid across the Boyne;
And you, who lately to your mother clung,
Have travelled far indeed for one so young.

Occasions of sin

There's retribution on the judgment day
For all who've led an innocent astray.
Each time I go to bed I think of that
And lock the butter out of reach of cat.

The book of life

Restored to favour, he's allowed to look
Over my shoulder while I read a book.
Some day, no doubt, I'll be no more than such,
And lucky if I understand as much.

On the demolition of Coole House

On that commanding slope
The prying picks dislodge
And split each brick from brick,
While at the water's edge
The bog-brown wavelets lap
Against the wet black rock.
But the water is gentle
Against its slippery flank
While toppling of overmantel
Lintel and jamb, are not:
The snapping of each link
Like thorns beneath the pot.

Such silence for so long
Was laid on that estate,
Laid upon every tongue
That came inside the gate,
No fool could call him friend
Nor a friend call him fool.
– The interdiction's end
Comes with the end of Coole.

The pictures in the gallery

The pictures in the gallery
Fade and are suddenly dark
The ancestors remember
The children in the park.

Under the scarlet banners
The candles have burnt low
And down the cold stone pathways
The children come and go

Backwards and forwards reading
Marble and granite names
Till nothing shows in darkness
But gilded picture frames.

Three epigrams

Footnote to XVIIIth-century literature

Dryden, Pope, Walpole, Gibbon, Chesterfield
  Knew well enough what forces kept at bay
The wild beasts from their cultivated field.
  In our remoter place and later day
        What now remains to check their fell advance
        In Holy Ireland, but one slender chance?

On the Casino at Clontarf

Lord Charlemont built this temple on the bog,
  And every night he slept in it, he knew
That crouching in the doorway slept the dog
  With one eye always open, often two.
        We have our little temples, but we own
        No guarantee that they'll be left alone.

A thought (in answer to Thomas Carew)

So, you have dug Love's grave at last,
And softly buried there, it moulders.
Don't let yourself be too downcast,
Think of the weight that's off your shoulders.

Poem for myself

As now in darkness I ascend the stair
At each return I look to find them cancelled –
The unanswered question left out in the square
And that which, asked by me, remains unanswered;
But no flame leaps across the loaded air.

Each turning insulated in the dark
Takes no account of the embracing structure:
Each episode on its own will raise a spark,
But between flashpoints there is no conductor.
We feel, like blind men, for an unlit mark.

Now that tomorrow is today, I take
For granted only this: on each occasion
All that we seek and do not find, we fake
Sooner or later, and the hesitation
That conscience prompts to, is the only brake.

I come down in the morning for the post
And do not find the half-expected letter.
The past is as irrevocably lost
As what can never happen, and it's better
To cut the loss than pay the mounting cost.

Whether asleep or risen from my bed
By night or day my private threshold's haunted
By the thin figures of the hungry dead.
By each some bodiless extraction's wanted
And I have nothing in the house but bread.

Sitting beside the fire alone

Sitting beside the fire alone
I conjure up more wicked shapes
Than ever crawled from under stone,
With knotted fingers, fur like apes,
Ears like elephants, beaks like storks,
Wings like bats and tails like forks.

Walking about the windy streets
With eyes on faces stones or bricks
I do not run to such conceits:
Imagination plays no tricks
Unless perhaps in playful pride
With one who walks them at my side.

Proverbial poem

And here am I, criss-crossed and cased with scars
Required again to peel away that mail,
And, stripped of all experience, plunge in
Naked as though newborn; no golden bars
Stored in the cellar lest the bank should fail.
Though nothing venture, surely nothing win,
I bear in mind how squalidly he begs
Who hawked a basket once too full of eggs.

Two voyages

I: Summer

Leaving the bar slack-watered, I have left
The quiet man in the corner with his pint
      Who did not speak, the hour
      We drank and chatted there.

High walls of granite overarched with elder
Dividing gardens. Long deserted lanes
      Behind the houses. Here
      The cats walk warily.

I walk with them to you, who like a cat
Sit curled and purr before an empty grate.
      Two points of light have hailed
      Each other in the night.

II: Winter

Love's equinoctial gales are past, the path
Along the long lanes leads again through night.
      The trees are bare, the air
      A halo round each lamp.

Gentlest imaginable groundswell heaving
Hardly disturbs the wrack. The wave that broke
      Over us both has passed
      And now the calm succeeds.

And now the fire's the focus of the room,
By winter made so. Like a gay salute
      There crackles in the hearth
      The holly's fusillade.

No climate for the vulture

Over the waking fields the air is moist;
Far-travelled hawks are circling in the air.
Your arms I leaned to, loading them with care
Have been the refuge where my trust was placed.

But body's lightness turns the heart to lead:
Imagination's function is reversed
Putting the last essential failure first
Before frustration's prelude is outplayed.

I look above the field, only to bid
Memory's hovering hawks return to nest
That do not feed on carrion, fearful lest
They swoop to find their prey already dead.

First winter

Back, like a tide of light, our summer dream
Flows in, converging on the hearth we call
Our own this winter. As a burning coal
Remits the payment long deferred in time
(Poured in, sealed up, encrusted thick with rime,
Thawed slowly out, but still remaining cool
Till it's touched off) – our buried capital
Bears interest again, flares forth as flame.

Circles are round, no matter where they're started:
Winter's no late time, spring no early one.
When the superfluous hearth is hollowest-hearted
Replenishment begins, and cunningly
The chairs, who know their parts better than we
Turn the cold shoulder there, and face the sun.

These grassy walks

These grassy walks are cool and light
And as I walk them now I light
A quiet Sunday-morning pipe
To fill the emptiness of sleep.

Tonight she will be sailing west
To the grey city, and farther west
The farmers and the islandmen
Smoke in the Sunday-morning sun.

Against rhetoric in love

Forgive me, dear, for letting you become
An easy groove, a habit of the mind,
Now that with lighter stroke is underlined
The factor that makes sense out of the sum.
Forgive me if, apparently at rest,
Indulging in one luxury, I leave
Unsaid some things you might perhaps believe,
Perhaps might not, and yet might wish expressed.

But here's your consolation, my excuse:
The mightiest arm was not designed for fighting.
To press the point too hard is nib's abuse
Nor adds one jot of cogency to writing,
And only relaxation can release
The final fountain of our private peace.

Although the lustre of your hair

Although the lustre of your hair
Admits no parallel except
The leaves before the wind has swept
Them off and left the branches bare,
There's nothing worth the fetching there;
Though they may counterfeit your gold
They're crisp as paper, light as air,
And moulder, though it be to mould.

The folds of foliage, heavily hung,
That frame your features as they do
(Though coloured like enough) are new
Because the year and you are young.
So hush the lithe ingenious tongue
And let the suns of summer shine
Wandering in and out among
The tendrils of the burnished vine.

Fire! Fire!

A red-gold head in the distance gleaming warm
Suggests in its colour and carriage the more than pretty;
And the moment before I am sure it is someone else
> Love like a fire-engine, bright with bells
> Brazenly shrilling, tears through the city
> Streets of my heart, on a false alarm.

Flowers upon your lips and hands

Flowers upon your lips and hands,
The gentle movement of your breast:
I have remembered these in lands
Where I was but a passing guest.

Strange, to have seen so long before,
Reflected through each flaw and fault,
This inlet on the sunlit shore
Where the sweet water meets the salt.

The kiss

Is then the difference so much
Between the other senses and the sense of touch,
That blindfold we presume to find
The nearest, most identical approach to mind?
That we ignore how many a slip
And fruitful source of error, lies twixt lip and lip?

Inside and out

Inside and out, that loveliness,
That fine-drawn skein of flesh and bone
Frightens me with a soft caress
So much, that now I am alone
I watch for every move I make:
A moment's tremor seems an hour,
As though one careless breath could shake
Each fragile petal from the flower.

Love-poem

Time has done thus to you and me:
Our lives' revolving discs are such
As make a figure of infinity
Always at one continuous point in touch.

With greater force and steadier yet
The meshes of the gears engage.
We are entangled in a liquid net,
We are imprisoned in a crystal cage.

Poem for Linde

My arms are round you now as we stand over
A lock of this canal, that with another
Embraces the dark city like a lover.

Soon against distant walls and windows thrown
Shadows of remembered beauty will walk round
The wide and level spaces of the town

To reinforce the insidious temptation
To change this moment's values into action
And offer you the insult of protection,

As if the negligible amount remaining
Of man's protective stature (and that fast waning)
Retained for such as us, one ounce of meaning.

Precarious and impermanent, we have
What but the frail revetment of our love
To match against what nightmare tidal wave?

So do not blame me that I have withheld
What might be given, being loth to build
Defences that, being so attacked, must yield.

A habit
or, **'Emotion recollected in tranquillity'**

That curious tendency she had – to push
   The head that shared with hers, right off the pillow –
Annoyed at times, but never made him wish
   She'd get herself a different bedfellow.
        Yet his head would not grudge the space denied it
        If it were sure another occupied it.

To his beloved on her having furnished his room with curtains

The stuffs that speak of you so gaily
Soften the rectilinear light
That stabbed in penetration daily:
– Now for the inner mode of sight.

You've draped the windows of my dwelling:
It still devolves on you to find
A will as constant and compelling
To drape the windows of my mind.

Yet there must always be a certain
Polarity twixt love and love.
The jamb is rigid behind the curtain;
Your soft hand fits my iron glove.

You whom I know

You whom I know,
Between whose mind and mine these currents flow
By which we keep, although apart,
A temperate climate in the heart,
You are my island's Gulf of Mexico.

All trafficking
And all transactions ultimately bring
Their merchandise into this port
With landfall-logs compressed, cut short
And stripped of every accidental thing.

You whom I keep
As underwriter, there to overleap
Refractive agents fixed between
The seer and the shifting scene,
Keep at me, that no sense may fall asleep.

Bombard my coast
With particles of warmth against the frost;
That into that stream all may flow,
Take on that current's grain, and so
Make, of each morsel in the mass, the most.

The false start

Ask it now, if you will, of those who stand
On balconies for the first time in the year.
Ask how they take the tentative approach
Of idle airs that coax the trees to bud
Gently and suddenly, across the road.

Some will confess to blood's uneasiness
At finding the year's curve deflected up
Abruptly, tasting shyly like a beast
The unfamiliar stimulus, each sense
Sharp with suspicion.
                              Others may let pass
(Being so regularly ground and wound
That nothing strange disturbs them) these mild skies,
The sweetness and the slightness of these winds,
With some stale stock remark that scarcely wakes
The lightly sleeping echo, lulled so long.

And some remain in whom the lost response
Is found and reinfused by conscious thought.
Double distrust restricts each breath they take:
The frost's behind them; and the frost in front
Threatens the shoots they watch, the shoots that push
Their tender spearheads in the long-tilled field,
Bright-pointed thoughts that spring so quick, so bright
That eyes that look direct see only sun.

Anticipation, retrospect, alone
Can dwell upon the lucid interval.
We lack the lithe resilience of the boughs
That bear the flowering blossom to the breeze.
The warmth and liquefaction of our earth
Dissolve, as well, the sense that should respond
As though the instant blurred our eyes with tears
And clarity of sight could only come
Before they flow, or after they have dried.

To the house of my hosts in October

The windfalls from your apple-trees
Fall thick on windy nights like these,
And like a sea-swept strand resound
The taller trees that stand around.

May every chance and lot that falls
Be fortunate, within your walls;
And may you breathe a peaceful air
Ring'd round by trees that speak you fair.

Marlay Park

6 May 1995

I stand on the platform
On a warm afternoon in May
Im wunderschönen Monat Mai
Shepherding little children
On to this miniature railway
Each for a three-minute ride.

I think of those who now
Would be fifty-five or sixty
And the clanging of the cattle-truck doors
And the clatter of couplings
And the chimneys beyond the wire,
And the piles of shoes.

A diary-entry versified

Now that the work of spade and plough is done
And merest copying by rote succeeds,
The small intrusive poems, one by one,
Come up like flowers the farmer counts as weeds.

Notes

After summer's ruin
The poem contains echoes of T.S. Eliot's quotation of the line *'Le Prince d'Aquitaine à la tour abolie'* from Gerard de Nerval's sonnet 'El Desdichado' ('The disinherited one') at the end of *The Waste Land* (1922).

Easter Tuesday 1941
The *Irish Times* for 15 April 1941 reported that Mr de Valera had reviewed 25,000 men in the 'Greatest Military Display for many years' as part of the annual Dublin celebrations of the Easter Rising of 1916.

diggers with both feet: 'to dig with the other (wrong) foot', a colloquial phrase used to indicate that someone is of a different religion, usually Protestant.

Kilcarty to Dublin, 1942
Kilcarty is a small Georgian house in County Meath, owned at the time of this poem by Maurice's friend Eoin Ó Beirne, a Canadian who lectured in law. See Maurice Craig's *Classic Irish Houses of the Middle Size* (2006 ed.), pp. 164-6.

Talk with an astronomer
The encounter came when Maurice was a volunteer night-watchman at the Cambridge University Institute of Astronomy during the war. The astronomer was Dr Hermann Bruch, an assistant in the observatory.

Georgian Dublin
Turgot: Jacques Turgot, Baron d'Aulne (1727-81), French economist and reforming minister of finance to Louis XVI, was the first economist to recognise the importance of time in economic transactions.

alembic: a flask for distilling and condensing liquids; *precipitates* are particles formed in liquid solutions during chemical reactions.

This Roman Empire refers to Ireland in the 'quick sunlight' of the period between Henry Grattan's declaration of Irish legislative independence from Britain in 1782 and the Act of Union of 1801.

Sedan refers both to the decisive Battle of Sedan (1870) in the Franco-Prussian war and to the use of sedan chairs in late-eighteenth-century Dublin.

Merrion Square: A descriptive poem
For James Ward's 'Phoenix Park', see *Miscellaneous Poems* ed. Matthew Concanen (London, 1724), pp. 379-91.

For details of the development of Merrion Square and the leases offered to developers, see Finola O'Kane, '"Bargains in view": the Fitzwilliam family's development of Merrion Square' in Christine Casey (ed.), *The Eighteenth-Century Dublin Town House: Form, Function and Finance* (Dublin, 2010), pp. 98-109.

The *Wide Streets Commissioners* were established in 1757. By the time this poem was written, most of the houses in Merrion Square had been turned into offices. The garden in the centre of the square is now a public park.

The religious order of the Sisters of Marie Reparatrice or Mary Reparatrix was founded in 1854 by a Belgian, Emilie d'Oultremont d'Hooghvorst.

The Irish writers who lived in Merrion Square were W. B. Yeats (1865-1939), George Russell (Æ) (1867-1935), Edward Martyn (1859-1923), George Moore (1852-1933) and Sheridan Le Fanu (1814-73). Sir Jonah Barrington (c.1760-1834), politician, barrister and author of revealing and entertaining memoirs, went into voluntary exile in Paris in 1810, accused of embezzling public funds.

Dun Laoghaire and Rathmines are Dublin suburbs.

A Civic Guard is a member of the Irish police force.

The lawn of *Leinster House*, originally the town house of the Dukes of Leinster, but now the seat of the Irish parliament, opens onto Merrion Square.

Gleams faint beyond an acre of Cathay. This line carries echoes of one from Tennyson's 'Locksley Hall': 'Better fifty years of Europe than a cycle of Cathay'. The *lesser* houses were in Kildare Place and have since been demolished.

Maurice's father came from Ballymoney, County Antrim.

Appointed to be sung in churches

The Psalms of David were twice rendered into rhyming stanzas 'appointed to be sung in churches'. The authors of the first version of these metrical psalms were Thomas Sternhold (d. 1549) and John Hopkins (d. 1570), and of the second Nahum Tate (1652-1714) and Nicholas Brady (1659-1726), both graduates of Trinity College Dublin.

Ballad to a traditional refrain

After they met in Paris in 1938, James Joyce asked Maurice if he could find the source of the line 'May the Lord in his mercy be kind to Belfast'. By the time Maurice had found the anonymous nineteenth-century ballad in which the line occurs, Joyce was dead. Subsequently, Maurice wrote his own ballad incorporating the traditional line; it has become the best known of his poems. See *The Elephant and the Polish Question* (1990), pp. 59-60.

In stanza three, the irony is that 'College Green' is not only the name of the street facing the Houses of the Irish Parliament in Dublin before 1800 (now the Bank of Ireland) but that it is also the name of the street beside Assembly's College, Belfast, where the Northern Ireland Parliament met between 1921 and 1932.

On the demolition of Coole House

Coole House, County Galway, home of Augusta Lady Gregory (1852-1932), was demolished in 1941. The second stanza of the poem refers to W. B. Yeats.

To the house of my hosts in October
The hosts were Geoffrey and Mary Taylor.

Marlay Park
In the 1990s, Maurice was a volunteer helping to run the miniature railway at
Marlay Park, Dublin.

'In the wonderful month of May' is the title of one of the songs in the cycle
Dichterliebe ('Poet's Love'), the words by Heinrich Heine (1797?-1856) and the music
by Robert Schumann (1810-56).